LIVING GREEN

Producing and Obtaining Food

WORLD
BOOK

a Scott Fetzer company

Chicago

www.worldbookonline.com

Editorial:

Editor in Chief: Paul A. Kobasa
Project Manager: Cassie Mayer
Writer: Ana Deboo
Editor: Brian Johnson
Researcher: Cheryl Graham, Daniel Kenis
Manager, Contracts & Compliance
 (Rights & Permissions): Loranne K. Shields
Indexer: David Pofelski

Graphics and Design:

Associate Director: Sandra M. Dyrlund
Manager: Tom Evans
Coordinator, Design Development
 and Production: Brenda B. Tropinski
Book design by: Don Di Sante
Designer: Matthew Carrington

Pre-Press and Manufacturing:

Director: Carma Fazio
Manufacturing Manager: Steve Hueppchen
Production/Technology Manager: Anne Fritzinger

World Book, Inc.
233 N. Michigan Avenue
Chicago, IL 60601
U.S.A.

For information about other World Book publications, visit our Web site at **http://www.worldbookonline.com** or call **1-800-WORLDBK (967-5325).**

For information about sales to schools and libraries, call **1-800-975-3250 (United States)**, or **1-800-837-5365 (Canada).**

Picture Acknowledgments:

Front Cover: © Cesare Gerolimetto, SIME/4Corners Images

© Aardvark/Alamy Images 50; © Eryrie/Alamy Images 8; © Eddie Gerald, Alamy Images 31; © Guenter Fischer, imagebroker/Alamy Images 4; © Vanessa Miles, Alamy Images 25; © Nic Miller, Organics Image Library/Alamy Images 1; © Stan Gamester, Photofusion/Alamy Images 27; © The Photolibrary Wales/Alamy Images 39; © Sinibomb/Alamy Images 51; © George Doyle, Stockbyte/Alamy Images 31; © Stock Italia/Alamy Images 40; © Pat Tuson, Alamy Images 54; © J. Marshall, Tribaleye/Alamy Images 7; © Ulrich Baumgarten, Vario/Alamy Images 36; © Juergen Moers, Vario/Alamy Images 35; AP/Wide World 13, 17, 19, 30; © Biosphoto/Peter Arnold, Inc. 38, 48; © Mark Edwards from Peter Arnold, Inc. 13; © Ron Giling from Peter Arnold, Inc. 49; © Alex S. Maclean from Peter Arnold, Inc. 12; © Jorgen Schytte from Peter Arnold, Inc. 10; © Bohemian Nomad Picturemakers/Corbis 24; © Barbar Walton/epa/Corbis 55; © Paul Ashton, SouthWest News Service/Sygma/Corbis 37; © Simon Rawles, Digital Railroad 33; © Joel Rogers, Digital Railroad 42; © Rob Badger and Nita Winter, Digital Railroad 32; © Veronique Krieger, DK Stock/Getty Images 52; © Michael Melford, Getty Images 17; © Doug Menuez, Photodisc/Getty Images 18; © Co Rentmeester, Time & Life Pictures/Getty Images 22; © Arthur Schatz, Time & Life Pictures/Getty Images 29; © Jeff Green, Reuters/Landov 15; © Jerzyworks/Masterfile 34; © Robert W. Ginn, Photo Edit 28; © Volker Steger, Photo Researchers 11; © Daniel Aguilar, Reuters 11; Satellite Imaging Corporation 21; © Shutterstock 5, 16, 37, 43, 46, 47, 53, 56, 58; © age fotostock/SuperStock 14, 43, 45; © Comstock/SuperStock 6; © Digital Vision/SuperStock 35; © UpperCut Images/SuperStock 26; © Whole Foods Market 23; © Wisconsin Potato & Vegetable Growers Association 9, 20; WORLD BOOK photo by Ted Shreshinsky 9; © Brian Smith, Telegraph UK/ZUMA Press 57.

All maps and illustrations are the exclusive property of World Book, Inc.

Library of Congress Cataloging-in-Publication Data

Producing and obtaining food.
    p. cm. -- (Living green)
  Includes index.
  Summary: "An exploration of the environmental, health, and social issues of modern agriculture. Features include fact boxes, sidebars, activities, glossary, list of recommended reading and Web sites, and index"--Provided by publisher.
  ISBN 978-0-7166-1409-8
  1. Agriculture--Environmental aspects--Juvenile literature. 2. Agriculture--Health aspects--Juvenile literature. 3. Agriculture--Social aspects--Juvenile literature. I. World Book, Inc. II. Series.
  S589.75.P77 2008
  630--dc22

2008035510

Living Green
Set ISBN: 978-0-7166-1400-5
Printed in China
2 3 4 5 6 13 12 11 10 09

Table of Contents

There is a glossary of terms on pages 60-61. Terms defined in the glossary are in type **that looks like this** on their first appearance in any section.

Introduction

Section Summary

Producing and obtaining food is vital to human survival. As the world's population increases, the amount of food we produce continues to grow. Many people are beginning to think about the environmental effects of food production.

"Green" foods are foods that are produced using methods that do not cause harm to the environment, to the people who eat the foods, or to the people who grow them. Making green food choices begins by learning more about the food we eat.

Even today, producing enough food to feed the world's people is of great global concern.

As the year 2000 approached, the global population reached 6 billion. It is estimated that by the year 2050, there will be more than 9 billion people in the world. All of these people will need a lot of food—and they are going to take up a lot of space. This is why, more and more, people are realizing that we need to **conserve** Earth's resources to make it possible for the planet to support everyone today and in the generations to come.

Some people are responding to this issue is by making "green" choices, which means doing things that benefit both the environment and society. The idea has been summed up in a catchy slogan: "Reduce, reuse, recycle"—sometimes called the "Three Rs" of the green movement. Examples of green choices include reusing items instead of throwing them away and recycling the trash you do generate. You might think twice about whether you really need to buy something, or you might choose a product made with recycled content or environmentally friendly materials.

What are green food choices?

Some people apply green principles to choosing the foods they eat. "Green" foods are produced using methods that minimize harm to the environment, to the people who eat the foods, and to the people who grow and process them. But how do you go about choosing green foods? Where do you find them, and how can you be sure you are making the best choices?

This is not always easy to figure out. There are many questions to ask yourself: Did the food travel far to get to you? What kinds of chemicals were used to grow it? How was the land treated? How were the farmworkers treated? How is the food packaged—is a lot of plastic used? Is the food affordable? After weighing these factors, you can set priorities to help you make the best possible choices from what's available in your area.

This book will help you to understand how different methods of food production affect the environment. It will help you make informed decisions when purchasing food. Each green decision you make contributes to improving the health of the planet. It may also influence other people to make green food choices. Ultimately, individual choices add up to powerful effects.

There are many questions to consider when making food choices.

What Is Conventional Agriculture?

Section Summary

Conventional agriculture describes the methods used by commercial farmers to grow large amounts of food as quickly as possible. These methods often include using human-made chemicals to help plants grow, planting only one type of crop, and using machines to break up soil to make it easier to grow crops.

Conventional farming methods have helped provide food for the world's people, but many of these methods can harm the environment.

Conventional farms rely on industrial machinery and chemicals to produce food.

Up until the mid-1800's, most people in the United States and other countries lived on small farms. Every member of the family worked on the farm, which required long hours of labor nearly every day of the week. Families grew vegetables and raised farm animals, often struggling to produce enough food for themselves.

Today, the number of small farms has shrunk dramatically. Most of the food sold at grocery stores comes from **commercial** farms that grow large amounts of food using conventional methods of agriculture. The term *conventional agriculture* describes practices that focus on producing a lot of food as quickly, efficiently, and profitably as possible. **Synthetic** chemicals may be used, such as **pesticides** and **fertilizers.**

Conventional agriculture employs methods associated with industrial mass production, such as planting large amounts of one type of crop or raising one kind of animal. In many ways, conventional agriculture follows the strategy people have always pursued: Use the most sophisticated methods available and make the work as manageable as possible.

Farming and early civilizations

Before people knew how to cultivate their own food, they had to search for edible plants and hunt animals for meat. This way of life is called hunting and gathering. Over time, however, people learned to grow certain plants and to raise animals. They learned to put part of their harvest into storage to get them through winter. This allowed them to settle down and live in one place all year. Life became easier and populations increased, which meant that more food was needed.

The Industrial Revolution

Early farmers used hand-held tools to tend to fields. Later, they hitched a horse, donkey, or ox to a wooden plow, a tool used to break up the soil for planting.

During the Industrial Revolution (1700's-1800's), a period when the lives and work of many people were changed by industrialization, agricultural machines replaced animals used for fieldwork. In the 1870's, the first steam-powered tractors became available. These machines pulled plows or other tools over land. By the 1920's, gasoline- or diesel-powered tractors and other tools made farm work faster and easier than ever before. Today, modern harvesting machines can do work that once required dozens of farmworkers.

At the same time that methods of producing food improved, a transportation revolution was underway. The invention of the steam-powered locomotive in the early 1800's led to the rapid development of railroads. By the mid-1800's, food could be sent in refrigerated compartments by **freight** train or ship to consumers hundreds or thousands of miles away.

Farming today

The 1900's brought the invention of synthetic chemicals to control pests and diseases that threaten crops. Synthetic fertilizers were invented to make plants grow faster and bigger.

Farming was long a small, family enterprise that fed local communities. Today, it has become profitable in a wider sense. Because more food could be produced and sent over long distances, there were many more potential customers than ever before. Gradually, big businesses took over the task of feeding much of the world.

The land dedicated to agriculture in the United States peaked in the 1950's at more than 1 billion acres (400 million hectares) of farmland. Since then, more than 250 million acres (101 million hectares) of this farmland have been lost, mainly to the spread of cities.

Some farmers still use oxen or other animals to pull wooden plows.

THE RISE OF AGRIBUSINESS

The system that has developed around conventional agriculture is known as **agribusiness.** The term includes not only the farms themselves but also the businesses related to agricultural production. These are:

- producers of **agrochemicals** (synthetic fertilizers and pesticides);
- manufacturers of farm equipment;
- food processors (such as grain mills or slaughterhouses);
- industrial kitchens that make prepared food items;
- companies that package food for sale;
- companies that market the food (promote it to consumers); and
- companies that do more than one of these things.

Cargill operates food plants around the world, such as this one in the United Kingdom.

One of the largest agribusinesses is Cargill, which started in 1865 as a grain warehouse in Iowa. Since then, it has expanded into nearly every branch of the food production process and has offices around the world. Among many other enterprises, Cargill makes feed for livestock (animals raised for food or other products); processes beef, pork, and poultry; and manufactures soy-based products, chocolate, malt for making beer, and sea salt. The company still stores grain, but it also grows, mills, and sells it in the United States and abroad. It is possible that on some days everything you eat has had something to do with Cargill. Other major agribusinesses include Archer Daniels Midland, Bunge Ltd., Monsanto, Nestle, and Unilever.

Increased food production

Modern agricultural methods and the development of agribusiness have made it possible to produce large amounts of food faster than ever before. Synthetic pesticides, **fungicides,** and **antibiotics** help to control damaging bugs and diseases. Sophisticated machinery makes it easier to cultivate fields, irrigate crops, and harvest and process food. Fertilizers make crops grow quickly. Special feed makes livestock mature faster.

The plants and animals farmers raise have been specially bred for conditions on the farm. Once harvested, fruits and vegetables resist spoiling. They are **hardy** enough to ship long distances. They make long-lasting, attractive displays in supermarkets.

Commercial farms often use irrigation and agrochemicals to grow crops.

Foods produced by large commercial farms are often cheaper than foods sold by small farms. This is partly because a large amount of food is grown so quickly by so few people. A large harvest can generate a significant profit even if the price is only slightly above the production cost. Thus, large commercial farms can make a profit on lower sales prices than small farms can.

Government involvement

Another factor that keeps prices low is the practice of giving agricultural **subsidies,** payments from the government that were originally intended to help farmers survive hard times. In the United States, subsidies were introduced in the 1930's as part of federal agricultural laws called **farm bills.** Over the years, the rules for subsidies have become extremely complicated. Farmers may produce so much of certain crops, such as corn, wheat, and soybeans, that the prices of those foods stay low. With so much hunger in the world, affordable food is an important goal. But critics say subsidies cause farmers to plant too much of the wrong crops and neglect the environment. They feel that with proper planning, farmers would need less government money.

A CLOSER LOOK
The Green Revolution
Industrial methods are credited for bringing food to millions. In the 1940's, a plant breeder named Norman Borlaug created a new variety of wheat that was disease-resistant, hardy, and very productive. He brought the new wheat to Mexico and later to other less developed countries. New varieties of crops grown with irrigation, fertilizer, and pesticides spurred a "Green Revolution" around the world. This Green Revolution has prevented famines in India and elsewhere in the decades since. Borlaug won the Nobel Peace Prize in 1970 for his work.

Norman Borlaug

GENETICALLY MODIFIED FOODS

Farming methods have not changed dramatically since the mid-1900's. However, the seeds planted by many farmers have changed. In the 1980's, scientists developed a way to directly alter the **genes** of crops to introduce beneficial characteristics. Genes are tiny parts of cells that help determine how an organism will look and function. **Genetically modified** foods, also called GM foods, can be altered for many purposes. Some crops are modified to make them more resistant to disease or pests, so they will require fewer pesticides. Others are modified to increase their taste, nutritional value, or shelf life. The United States is the leading producer of GM foods today.

Scientists use modern lab techniques to create genetically modified foods.

GM foods first became widely available in the 1990's. During this time, scientists discovered that they could use genetic engineering to transfer traits from **bacteria** to plants. The plants then became poisonous to the same insects that the bacteria kills. This kind of corn has been extremely successful. It was first introduced in 1996. By 2007, it accounted for 49 percent of the corn crop in the United States.

Selective breeding and GM foods

Though GM foods are relatively new to agriculture, the principle of selectively breeding crops or animals has been used by farmers for thousands of years. If a farmer noticed that a particular group of tomatoes were hardier than other groups, he or she could select seeds from those tomatoes and plant them the next year. All domestic animals, such as pets and farm animals, are also the result of selective breeding. Most of these plants and animals would have trouble surviving in the wild.

While selective breeding involves guiding natural processes, the production of GM foods involves wholly artifical methods. Using modern lab techniques, scientists take genes from one organism and put them into another. The organisms may be largely unrelated to each other, such as bacteria and corn.

Advantages of GM foods

Supporters of GM foods emphasize improvements in crop harvests, with the potential for more improvements. Crops that repel

bugs and diseases need fewer industrial pesticides. Plants could be engineered to grow in places where they could not otherwise survive. This could reduce clearing such areas as rain forests for agriculture. It could also bring agriculture to deserts in less developed countries, where hunger is common.

Critics worry about the effects genetically modified crops might have in the wild.

Plants can be modified to contain important nutrients, even medicines. In 1999, scientists engineered Golden Rice to produce vitamin A. Vitamin A deficiency can cause birth defects and night blindness, among other problems. Many of the world's poorest people would benefit. However, safety concerns have stalled Golden Rice. By 2008, Golden Rice was being tested in some countries but had not yet been approved for release.

Disadvantages of GM foods

Critics of GM foods fear that they could have unexpected effects. What happens if the genetically modified organisms escape into the wild? Could they crowd out native plants or harm insects and animals? Would they create pesticide-resistant bugs and weeds? Some critics worry that GM foods could cause more immediate problems. For example, what if a person eats a food that contains genes from a plant to which he or she is allergic?

Many critics recognize GM foods' promise but want to investigate potential problems. They also insist that GM foods be marked so consumers know what they are buying, which is not yet required in the United States. Supporters of such GM foods as Golden Rice reply that delays cost lives.

A CLOSER LOOK
Food Nanotechnology

Nanotechnology is the science of creating substances by combining individual atoms and molecules—building blocks so tiny that you can see them only through powerful microscopes. Scientists are investigating how nanotechnology can be applied to food. Currently, there is a version of canola cooking oil that blocks absorption of harmful cholesterol, a vitamin-enriched chocolate shake, and a tea that boosts immunity (resistance to disease). Researchers are working on many others, including fatty foods that do not cause weight gain.

People are beginning to ask the same questions about foods created using nanotechnology that they ask about GM foods, such as whether these foods are safe to eat and how they may affect the environment.

Nanotechnology laboratory

ENVIRONMENTAL EFFECTS OF CONVENTIONAL AGRICULTURE

Despite their successes, many conventional methods of producing food have proved to have disadvantages over time. Most problems have to do with the burdens placed on the environment as the land is cleared, plowed, and cultivated year after year. Many of the agrochemicals used on conventional farms pose threats to wildlife, as well as the health of farmworkers and consumers.

Tilling fields can cause large amounts of topsoil to be carried away by wind.

Eroded soil

Early on, farmers discovered that **tillage** is a helpful method of farming. Tillage is the process of breaking up **topsoil** using a plow or other tool, such as a hoe. The process leaves the dirt crumbly instead of packed hard. It is easier to get seeds into tilled ground. Plowing also controls weeds and turns under the debris from past crops. The broken-up dirt allows more oxygen to reach the roots of the plants, which helps them to grow.

Unfortunately, the loose dirt can dry out and get blown around by wind or washed away by rain—a process known as **erosion.** The dirt that runs off the fields can contaminate nearby water sources. It takes between 300 and 1,000 years for an inch (2.54 centimeters) of topsoil to accumulate. On land cleared for farming, that could all wash away in just a few heavy rainstorms.

Deforestation

When people cut down or burn forests, it is called **deforestation.** Larger areas of farmland are needed as the world's population grows. In less developed countries, this threatens forests. Many impoverished **subsistence farmers** use the ancient **slash-and-burn** method of agriculture. With this method, farmers cut down trees and burn underbrush to clear land for crops. The ash from such burning provides rich nutrients for the soil. However, these nutrients soon get depleted (used up), so the farmers move to new land, where they repeat the process.

Attracted by the inexpensive labor and land in less developed countries, agribusinesses have introduced large-scale agriculture to these areas. Worldwide, tropical rain forests, such as the Brazilian Amazon and the Lacandan in Mexico, as well as forests in Vietnam, Malaysia, and central Africa, are shrinking rapidly. As a result, many animal and plant species are becoming extinct. Bare land is vulnerable to erosion and the effects of flooding. In some regions, desert may soon replace cleared forest.

Deforestation has another damaging impact. It contributes to **global warming**, or an increase in Earth's surface temperature. Scientists believe that the build-up of **carbon dioxide** and other gases is the main cause of global warming. These gases collect in the **atmosphere** and trap the sun's heat, much like a greenhouse. Scientists call this the **greenhouse effect** and such gases as carbon dioxide **greenhouse gases.** Plants absorb carbon dioxide from the air. Thus, when large areas of forests are cleared, more carbon dioxide collects in the atmosphere. Burning forests to clear land also releases carbon dioxide stored by the trees and other plants.

In **industrialized countries**, deforestation is already largely complete. In the United Kingdom, farmers began the process at least 5,000 years ago. By 1870, most of the United Kingdom's woods had disappeared—only 5 percent of the original area remained. In the United States, much of the forests east of the Mississippi River were gone by the mid-1800's. People have made some progress in restoring forests in the developed world. Today, urban sprawl (spreading cities) is a more serious threat to forests than farming in such areas.

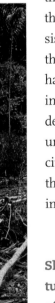

Slash-and-burn agriculture destroys huge areas of forest each year.

A CLOSER LOOK
The Dust Bowl

In the early 1900's, farmers across the Great Plains cleared large areas of land and tilled them heavily without trying to preserve the moisture in the soil. In the 1930's, a serious drought came, along with strong winds. In these conditions, the dry, dusty topsoil simply blew off the fields. Sometimes the dust in the air was so thick that the sky became dark. People called these dust storms "black blizzards." During this time, the region became known as the Dust Bowl. Unable to farm, and suffering in the hostile environment, many people left their homes. The situation did not improve until the following decade, when the drought ended and farmers began to use methods that reduce erosion.

A dust storm

Workers exposed to agrochemicals may suffer a number of health problems.

Use of agrochemicals

The chemicals used in conventional agriculture can dramatically improve farmers' results, but these substances also have negative effects. For example, fertilizers are chemicals that are used to strengthen crops. These chemicals slowly run through the soil and collect in nearby water sources, where they act as nutrients for algae (plantlike organisms). The algae then begin to reproduce more frequently. As the algae die, bacteria in the water use oxygen to carry out decomposition. Reduced oxygen levels cause many water-living organisms to die. This process is called **eutrophication.**

Pesticides, which include **insecticides**, **herbicides**, and fungicides, are chemicals that can kill harmful organisms. However, spraying pesticides onto crops releases potentially dangerous chemicals into the air, where they can be breathed in by farmworkers. If wind catches the airborne particles, they can affect plants and animals that live far from farmers' fields.

A famous example of a problem with agricultural chemicals is the synthetic insecticide DDT. During World War II (1939-1945), DDT was used to kill disease-carrying body lice and mosquitoes. It saved many lives. After the war, farmers used it to control insects. In time, biologist Rachel Carson discovered that in areas where DDT was used, bird numbers had plunged. She discovered that the chemicals in DDT had made the birds' egg shells too thin to protect the developing chicks. Carson revealed her findings in the book *Silent Spring* in 1962. Since then, many countries, including the United States, have made DDT illegal.

Use of hormones and antibiotics

In the United States, many dairy farmers give cows the **hormone** called rBGH (recombinant bovine growth hormone) to make them produce more milk. The safety of this synthetic hormone is debated, and it is banned in many areas, including the **European**

Union and Canada. Many people worry that it contaminates the milk. They note that rBGH increases udder infections and other problems in cows, which may contaminate the milk with pus and antibiotics. They also argue that elevated hormone levels in milk may cause cancer. Agribusinesses, the U.S. Food and Drug Administration (FDA), and some scientists dispute these claims.

Antibiotics are used to prevent or cure infectious diseases caused by **microbes**. Such illnesses can spread quickly among animals that are crowded together, as they often are on large farms. Antibiotics are also added to livestock feed to make animals grow larger.

Antibiotics have saved many lives since they were discovered, but the more often bacteria are exposed to antibiotics, the likelier they are to develop resistance to them. Today, many bacteria are becoming immune to antibiotics. Some people worry that farmers use too many antibiotics. They fear that this may create and spread infections that do not respond to medication.

Many modern farms treat cows with growth hormones and antibiotics.

Large commercial farms require much water and energy to grow crops.

Energy and water use

As conventional agriculture has made greater use of modern technology, its consumption of such resources as energy and water has increased. **Fossil fuels** (oil, coal, and natural gas) are needed to power such machinery as tractors and harvesters; to process, package, and store foods (often under refrigeration); and to ship them to markets around the world. It takes an especially large amount of energy to manufacture such chemical inputs as fertilizers. Producing fertilizers accounts for about 30 percent of all the energy used in conventional agriculture.

Fossil fuels are **nonrenewable resources**—that is, supplies of them are limited and will one day run out. Moreover, fossil fuels must be burned in order to release their energy. Burning fossil fuels releases carbon dioxide and pollution in the form of smoke, **carbon monoxide**, and other harmful substances. Some of these substances contribute to global warming, increasing temperatures within Earth's atmosphere.

Growing plants or raising animals also requires large amounts of water. The larger a farm, the more water it typically needs. Rainfall can rarely be counted on to provide enough water at the right time, so it is usually necessary to irrigate the land, bringing in water from streams, rivers, lakes, or from beneath the earth.

About one-third of the water used in the United States is used for irrigation. That figure is closer to 90 percent in some parts of the world, such as Mexico and India. In dry areas or during times of drought, there is not enough water for farms. Sometimes, people and farms must compete for water. Some rivers and lakes have dried up completely due to irrigation, causing enormous damage. Diverting rivers by building dams in order to store and redistribute water also causes environmental damage.

Creation of monocultures

As demand for certain products increases, many large farms begin focusing on just one kind of crop or livestock. This approach, known as **monoculture,** is easier because all the equipment and supplies used, as well as the jobs to be done, can be targeted for that one product. But it also causes problems. Groups of a single plant or animal are more vulnerable to diseases. The soil becomes depleted if the same crop is grown year after year, so more agrochemicals must be used. Monocultures can also devastate wildlife. When only one type of crop is planted, the animals, plants, and microbes in the soil that relied on other plants cannot survive. People's diet also becomes less varied. More than half of the plant-based foods people eat come from just four crops: wheat, corn, rice, and potatoes.

Monocultures, such as these wheat fields in Montana, can devastate wildlife.

A CLOSER LOOK
Almonds and Bees

The case of California almond orchards is an example of how monocultures disrupt natural processes. About 80 percent of the world's almonds are produced in California, where the orchards cover about 1,000 square miles (2,590 square kilometers). There are few native bees in California because bees need other sources of nectar when the almonds are not blooming. Without pollination, there will be no nuts, so almond growers rent bees.

Every February, about 40 billion bees are transported to California from all over the country. In recent years, a mysterious disease called colony collapse disorder has killed large numbers of them. Experts fear that bringing bees together every year is allowing the disease to spread.

Section Summary

Sustainable agriculture involves growing food in a way that supports the environment. Examples of sustainable agricultural methods include switching the types of crops grown from year to year and using natural substances to control pests.

Sustainable methods may be more time-consuming than conventional agricultural methods. Some critics wonder whether these methods can produce enough food to feed the world's population. Supporters of sustainable agriculture argue that conventional agriculture damages the soil, which eventually decreases the amount of crops that can be grown.

Sustainable agriculture involves growing food in ways that preserve the natural environment.

What Is Sustainable Agriculture?

The problems with conventional methods have inspired people to think about how to make agriculture less damaging to the environment. **Sustainable agriculture** involves producing food in ways that sustain, or support, Earth's natural environment. Many farmers recognize the drawbacks to conventional methods. They are willing to switch to **sustainable** practices that are effective and profitable. Common sustainable farming techniques include crop rotation, **conservation tillage**, **integrated pest management**, and the use of biologically-based substitutes for **agrochemicals**.

Crop rotation

Crop rotation involves changing what is grown in a field so that each planting helps repair the negative effects of the one that came before it. Corn, soybeans, and alfalfa are frequently used in crop-rotation plans. Corn takes the chemical element nitrogen from the soil, which all plants need in order to grow. Then soybeans and alfalfa are planted to replace the nitrogen.

Crop rotation is an ancient practice, but the rise of **synthetic fertilizers** in the 1900's seemed to make it unnecessary. Farmers benefitted from planting only the most valuable crops year after year. It turns out that crop rotation still has advantages, though. Done properly, it can increase crop yields while reducing the need for expensive, potentially harmful chemicals. Because it is not always necessary to plow after a harvest, **erosion** is less of a problem. Pests that threaten one crop may not be attracted by the others and may leave the area.

Conservation tillage

Conservation tillage limits plowing in order to prevent erosion and water loss. The term covers varying practices, from low-till (some plowing is done, but the remains of the last crop are left on at least 30 percent of the surface) to no-till (the farmer does not plow at all). One approach, called strip tillage or ridge tillage, alternates narrow, cleared strips of land where the seeds are planted with unplowed, unplanted strips.

After a harvest, farmers using conservation tillage leave the remains of the crop in the fields. They may also plant a **cover crop**, such as ryegrass, to protect and nourish the soil. When they plant again, they insert the seeds into the ground through the layer of natural debris. Keeping the moist **topsoil** in place reduces soil erosion. It improves yields and requires less fertilizer. Farmers save time, and they use less fuel to power farm equipment. Conservation tillage ultimately saves farmers money.

In 2007, about two-thirds of all farmland in the United States was cultivated using some form of conservation tillage. Only about one-third was still tilled using conventional practices.

Some machinery, such as this no-till drill, can reduce erosion and the need for fertilizers.

Healthy Grown potatoes from Wisconsin are grown using a strict pest management strategy.

ALTERNATIVES TO SYNTHETIC CHEMICALS

Farmers wishing to cause less environmental damage have sought ways to grow healthy plants with minimal use of synthetic chemicals, such as **pesticides** or fertilizers. Alternatives to synthetic chemicals vary, from the do-it-yourself methods of integrated pest management to the use of natural chemicals.

Integrated pest management

Integrated pest management (IPM) is a many-part approach to controlling threats to crops. The goal is to use as few harmful synthetic pesticides as possible, so other tactics are tried first. These tactics might include planting crops that are resistant to a certain pest, releasing natural predators of the pest, rotating crops, and using natural chemicals.

If all else fails, high-tech methods can help determine when and where to apply pesticides to achieve the greatest result with the smallest doses. A farmer might even calculate that the damage a pest can cause will be less expensive than fighting it. In that case, it might be better to do nothing.

Healthy Grown brand potatoes, from Wisconsin, are an example of successful and profitable IPM use by conventional farmers. The potatoes result from a collaboration among the Wisconsin Potato and Vegetable Growers Association, the University of Wisconsin, the World Wildlife Fund, and other **conservation** organizations. Together, these groups developed a strict IPM strategy. A separate organization, Protected Harvest, was created to **certify** the potatoes produced by farmers who enrolled in the program to follow the Healthy Grown standards. Protected Harvest has been profitable enough to convince about 10 percent of the potato farmers in the state to participate.

There are three basic types of biologically produced pesticides, called **biopesticides**:

- biochemicals, or chemicals that come from natural materials;
- microbial pesticides, which contain such **microbes** as **bacteria**; and
- plant-incorporated protectants, or plant varieties that have been **genetically modified** to resist pests.

In general, biopesticides don't last as long synthetic pesticides, because they tend to decompose (break down) into harmless substances. They can also often be targeted to specific pests, rather than striking across a broad range. That makes them safer for the environment and for the people who come into contact with them.

The most commonly used biopesticide is the microbial **insecticide** Bt, short for *Bacillus thuringiensis*. It is made from insect-repellent bacteria that live in some kinds of soil. The insecticide comes in several varieties that target different problem insects, such as cabbageworms, European corn borer larvae (young insects), and Colorado potato beetles. Bt is toxic only if it is eaten by the bugs in their larval stage and dissolved during digestion.

Challenges of sustainable agriculture

Devising effective sustainable methods and convincing farmers to use them are significant challenges. Most conventional methods came about because they were effective, affordable, and easy to implement. Sustainable methods may be more time-consuming. Farmers may have to learn new approaches and buy different equipment. Some farmers question whether biopesticides are really safer. They also question whether these methods can produce enough food in a world that now needs so much of it.

One method being developed to make farming more sustainable relies on sophisticated technology. Precision agriculture is the result of research by scientists at the U.S. National Aeronautics and Space Administration and other organizations. It uses satellite data to evaluate soil conditions and crop growth. With this information, farmers can apply the minimum amount of chemicals to only certain parts of a field. Similarly, they can add more water to only dry spots in fields. Such technology saves farmers time and money while helping to preserve the environment.

Satellite image of a farm in Saudi Arabia

THE ORGANIC MOVEMENT

An increasingly common response to controversies surrounding the use of synthetic chemicals and **genetically modified** foods is to avoid both. This is the strictest way of approaching sustainable farming practices. It is known as **organic** agriculture. Organic agriculture emphasizes following the cycles of nature as closely as possible, rather than trying to control these processes.

Some people believe that organic foods, such as these sunflower seeds, are safer for human consumption than conventionally grown varieties.

Until the early 1900's, all farmers' methods were essentially organic. Technology had not advanced enough to provide farmers with the machines and chemicals necessary for conventional farming. As industrial farming methods became more common, a number of people observed the changes with concern. In 1905, the British agricultural expert Sir Albert Howard was working in India and noticed that the soil there was more **fertile** than in the United Kingdom. The plants and livestock were not as vulnerable to diseases. Guessing that the farmers' age-old methods were responsible, Howard investigated further and became convinced. His book, *An Agricultural Testament* (1940), is the basis for many ideas important to organic farmers today.

While Howard was conducting research, Jerome I. Rodale began working to develop and promote organic agricultural practices in the United States. He founded the Rodale Institute to research ways to improve farming and gardening. He also founded the Rodale Press to publish books about the topic.

At first, the organic movement was small-scale and entirely local. Beginning in the 1960's, more people became interested in "health foods." Grocery stores began carrying foods labeled "organic," but there was no standard for what that meant.

To fix this, the United States Congress passed the Organic Foods Production Act with the 1990 **farm bill.** Under this law, which took effect in 2002, the National Organic Program (NOP)

USDA ORGANIC

was created as part of the U.S. Department of Agriculture (USDA). The NOP oversees procedures to be followed before food can be labeled organic. These include using IPM and working to prevent problems before they become difficult to manage. The use of synthetic chemicals must be minimal.

As a last resort, farmers may use synthetic substances named in a special list. For instance, certain alcohols may be used as disinfectants. The list also prohibits using some natural substances, among them the poison arsenic. Before a field can be used for organic crops, it must be kept free of forbidden chemicals for at least three years. For meat products to be labeled organic, livestock must eat only certified organic feed.

Similar standards for organic certification exist in the **European Union**, Japan, Canada, and other parts of the world. International organizations, such as the Germany-based International Federation of Organic Agriculture Movements (IFOAM), work to establish global standards that will make it easier for countries to trade organic goods.

If the front label says...	It means...
100% Organic	Grown and processed using only the approved materials and methods.
Organic	Contains at least 95 percent organic ingredients; processed by a certified handler.
Made with Organic Ingredients	70 percent or more of the ingredients are organic.
Certified Naturally Grown (CNG) or Biodynamic Certification	Certified by a private organization. (The standards for both CNG and Demeter, which issues Biodynamic certification, call for organic practices.)

Also...

• It is not mandatory for the actual USDA organic logo to be used. You may find information about certification elsewhere on the label.

• If the package does not say "organic," the food might still have some organic ingredients. These will be noted in the ingredients list.

Health food stores, such as Whole Foods Market, carry a number of organic foods. You can use the chart on this page to learn more about what the various organic labels mean.

These raspberry fields are part of Cascadian Farm in Washington state.

THE GROWTH OF ORGANIC AGRIBUSINESS

As the organic movement has gained popularity, many organic farms have gone from small, family-run organizations to large **agribusinesses**. Cascadian Farm is an example of an organic farm that made the transition from the early, small-scale days of the movement to the big business organic food has become.

Gene Kahn founded the farm in 1972 in Washington state. At first, he sold produce at local health-food stores and **cooperatives**. Steadily, the business expanded to become national, adding such prepared foods as jams, frozen fruits, and organic frozen entrees. In 1997, Kahn co-founded Small Planet Foods, which brought together Cascadian Farm, Muir Glen organic tomato growers, and Fantastic Foods, an organic vegetarian product line. By this time, organic foods were so profitable that they had attracted the attention of agribusinesses. Small Planet was bought by General Mills in 2000, though Cascadian Farm is still under Kahn's supervision. He was also active in helping to establish the U.S. Department of Agriculture (USDA) standards for organic production.

Some farmers who use organic methods prefer to stay small and local. For them, the process of obtaining government certification may involve too much time-consuming paperwork and expense. The Organic Foods Production Act allows farms that sell less than $5,000 worth of organic food a year to call their produce organic without certification, although they cannot use the certified-organic logo on packages. Uncertified farms that sell more than that amount must come up with another way to describe their foods.

One alternative to USDA certification is provided by an organization called Certified Naturally Grown (CNG). It was created especially for small farmers and seeks to provide strict standards along with a certification procedure. The agricultural practices required are organic, although that term cannot be used. If approved, instead of displaying the USDA logo on packages, farmers use the CNG logo. In the United Kingdom, the Wholesome Food Association provides a similar service to small farmers.

Some organic farmers object to the USDA law for various reasons. Some fear that USDA's organic regulations will be too difficult to enforce on a large scale and some ineligible foods may be labeled organic.

Many smaller farmers decide they do not need organic certification for one reason or another. By selling locally, at farm stands or farmers' markets, they can speak directly with their customers and explain their methods without having to use the organic label.

Workers harvest organic lettuce in the United Kingdom.

EXAMINING ORGANIC FOODS

There is much debate about whether organic foods are better than conventional ones, with strong feelings on both sides. Research into the health benefits of organic foods is ongoing. Meanwhile, organic farmers continue to improve their methods. Such efforts may convince critics in time.

Many grocery stores now feature organic produce sections.

Environmental effects

Organic farms consistently have lower chemical **residues** in their soil and crops, as well as increased **biodiversity**. Livestock are generally healthier. Critics doubt organic methods are practical for large-scale production, but supporters argue that they can be.

Pollution remains a problem. **Fossil fuels** and electricity still power equipment and facilities on organic farms. An organic farmer who has greenhouses must use energy for heating. When organic crops are made into processed foods, the energy required is comparable to processing conventional foods. Often, less energy is needed for organic cultivation. Organic farmers plow less and use fewer synthetic chemicals, which require much fuel to manufacture. However, sometimes organic farms may use more fossil fuel. For example, organically raised chickens take longer to mature, potentially requiring more energy per chicken.

Nutritional value and taste

Many people are convinced that organic foods taste better, but flavor is difficult to study. So much affects it, such as personal preference, the food's age, and how it was stored. A project at Washington State University tried to control these factors. Researchers grew the same kind of apples using organic, conventional, and combination methods. Taste-testers preferred the organic apples.

Promising nutritional research includes work by a scientist named Anne-Marie Mayer. She analyzed data from British produce collected over 60 years starting in the 1930's, when farming was essentially organic. Mayer found that nutrient levels fell over time and suggested that this might be linked to the adoption of **conventional agriculture.** In 2007, scientists in California found that organic tomatoes had much higher levels of beneficial substances called flavonoids. A 2008 report by the Organic Center reviewed many studies and concluded that organic foods are generally more nutritious. For example, when comparing the two versions of the same foods, the organic one contained more vitamin C about 50 percent of the time.

For some people, it is enough that organic foods are exposed to fewer synthetic chemicals than conventionally grown food. Critics question whether the chemical traces in conventional foods are harmful. Some critics suggest that manure used as fertilizer makes organic food dangerous because the manure could contain harmful *E. coli* bacteria, though this danger has not yet been proved.

Cost and availability

Organic foods cost more—sometimes much more—than conventional ones. This is because production takes more time and labor, and the farmers do not benefit from **subsidies.** There are also fewer organic choices available, although this may change if more people decide that organic foods are worth the extra cost. Some **environmentalists** argue that if organic food is healthier, consumers may save money because they will ultimately spend less on medical care.

Organic tomatoes contain high levels of beneficial flavonoids.

Section Summary

The social issues of agriculture involve the treatment and pay of farmworkers. Since farm work comes and goes with the seasons, many farmers hire temporary workers at harvest time. These workers may come from other countries. Pay is often poor, and working conditions can be dangerous.

Many people argue that sustainable farming must address social issues. They feel that all farmworkers should receive fair treatment and pay.

The Social Issues of Agriculture

Migrant workers pack harvested strawberries in Florida.

Some people who study agriculture believe that large farms cannot be considered fully **sustainable** unless they address the treatment of farmworkers, as well as the methods used to grow food. Workers should be fairly paid and their safety should be assured. The community that includes the farm should also benefit.

Worker conditions

Farm work presents a unique challenge for employers because it is seasonal. At harvest time, there is often much more to be done than workers can handle. During winter, there may be work for only a few people. Because of this, many farmers hire migrant laborers, who work at the busiest times and then move on. **Migrant labor** is not highly paid, and the workers cannot settle down to make a home. Many migrant laborers are immigrants, who must support themselves however they can in a foreign country.

Agriculture is consistently rated one of the most dangerous industries by the National Institute for Occupational Safety and

Health, part of the U.S. Centers for Disease Control. The dangers include respiratory ailments and skin diseases caused by chemicals and dust. Workers risk poisoning by **pesticides.** Farming involves hard physical labor, and workers may suffer skin cancer or heatstroke caused by overexposure to the sun. Often, farming requires the use of heavy machinery. About 100 people are killed each year when tractors overturn.

In less developed countries, conditions for workers can be even more difficult. Many farmers barely survive on what they earn. Education about using agricultural chemicals safely may not be available, or the safety equipment may be too costly. In some cases, chemicals that are banned in **industrialized countries** are still used in less developed countries.

The United Farm Workers of America, a **labor union** founded in the 1960's by the activists Cesar Chavez and Dolores Huerta, helped draw attention to the farms' working conditions. Still, many troubles remain, and they are not exclusive to **conventional agriculture.** The work on sustainable farms also comes and goes, and pay can be low. Fewer harmful chemicals are used, but that can also mean that more physical labor, such as weeding, is required. In the United States, **organic** farms are not required to meet standards for working conditions.

Farmworkers in other industrialized countries have similar problems. The International Union of Food and Agriculture Workers, an organization based in Switzerland, sets standards of treatment for migrant laborers in the **European Union.**

Among the groups working to find solutions to the problems of world food production and social injustice are the Food and Agriculture Organization (FAO), part of the **United Nations,** and the International Federation of Organic Agriculture Movements (IFOAM). IFOAM's standards for international **certification** of organic foods include provisions for workers' rights. The Fairtrade Labelling Organization (FLO), based in Germany, sets standards for working conditions and certifies qualifying foods.

Labor activist Cesar Chavez, center, fought to improve conditions for farmworkers.

The Social Issues of Agriculture 29

Making Green Food Choices

Section Summary

Making green food choices requires estimating the environmental impact of food items. This involves many factors, such as the distance the food traveled and whether human-made chemicals were used to grow it.

Making green food choices is not always simple. For example, a food may require much energy to produce, but it might also add nutritional value to your diet. Sometimes foods that are grown organically may be too expensive to fit into your budget. Knowing more about food production can help you make the right choices for both you and the environment.

Producing a simple bag of potato chips requires a surprising amount of energy.

There are a lot of things you can do to make your food choices as green as possible. The overall environmental impact of doing something—bringing a food "from farm to fork," as many people say—is expressed in various ways. **Embodied energy** describes the total amount of energy required to produce and market something. A **carbon footprint** is the amount of **carbon dioxide** released into the **atmosphere** in the process. **Food miles** expresses the distance the food must travel to get to market.

When making green food choices, it is important to think about the processes that were involved in producing that type of food. It is easy to forget, while eating a bag of potato chips, that those chips were once plants in a field. It takes a lot to transform raw potatoes into a crispy, packaged snack.

As part of a plan to begin reducing energy usage, the British potato-chip manufacturer Walkers calculated the amount of carbon dioxide released as the ingredients for a 1.2-ounce (34.5-gram) bag of cheese-and-onion-flavored chips were grown, processed, packaged, and transported. They also calculated how much carbon dioxide was released by disposing of the empty bag. In 2007, this released 2.6 ounces (75 grams) of **greenhouse gases**, about twice the weight of the chips. Forty-four percent of that came from growing and harvesting the potatoes, so processing and packaging accounted for more than half the gas released.

Processed foods

Highly processed foods may contain many chemicals. These are often added to pre-

Foods packaged in plastic may have an added environmental impact.

serve food, color it, make it a certain texture, or add flavor. Manufacturing **additives** increases a food's embodied energy, and they might not be good for you. For example, some nutritional scientists suggest avoiding an additive called *butylated hydroxyanisole*, or BHA. It is used to keep potato chips and other crisp foods tasting fresh, but it might increase the risk of cancer.

For most experts, the biggest worry is how processed foods may affect people's weight. Today, the rate of obesity in the United States is twice as high as in the 1970's, and now one in three people is seriously overweight. It can be easier to gain weight eating processed foods. They can taste satisfying without meeting the body's nutritional needs, which can cause you to crave more food.

If you wish to avoid highly processed foods, check the ingredients list on food labels. If it is long and contains many unfamiliar terms, the food is likely to be highly processed.

Food packaging

When buying a packaged food, pay attention to the packaging material. Simply packaged foods usually carry less embodied energy than items that include multiple layers of wrapping. Ideally, if there is a package at all, it should be made from recyclable materials, such as cardboard, glass, or metal. Certain kinds of plastic are recyclable in some areas, but most plastic food packaging cannot be recycled. You can also check the product's label to see if they used recycled materials for the packaging.

A CLOSER LOOK
Corn and Your Diet

Many food products sold in the United States are in some way related to corn. Most meat comes from animals that were fed corn. Corn is also used to make oil, among other products. One common corn product is a sweetener called high fructose corn syrup, or HFCS. Fructose is a sugar, and sugars are carbohydrates, which provide us with energy. However, too much sugar in the diet can cause tooth decay and weight gain. Because it is more affordable, HFCS has replaced sugar in many foods. HFCS is even in things that do not taste sweet, such as salad dressing and ketchup. To find out if HFCS is in the products you buy, read the ingredients label.

Locally grown foods can be better for the environment than foods shipped long distances.

Locally grown foods

Buying from local farms is a great way to reduce your environmental impact. Local food often has less embodied energy than food that must travel long distances. It is also fresher. An added benefit is that you support your community.

Some people try to eat only foods grown or raised within a set distance from their home, usually ranging from 50 to 150 miles (80 to 241 kilometers). They call themselves locavores. However, in some regions, it can be extremely difficult to find a healthful variety of foods the year around.

Fair trade foods

You can also consider ethical issues when purchasing foods. Bananas, pineapples, and mangoes are tropical fruits that are mostly grown in less developed countries. However, you can decide to buy the brands that have **fair trade certification.** This label indicates that farmworkers were paid a suitable wage for their work.

Weighing the options

People who have tried to pinpoint the greenest food practices have found that there are no straightforward answers. For example, although buying locally produced foods is generally considered a green practice, local food does not always have the lowest embodied energy.

In 2006, a group of researchers compared the embodied energy of locally grown apples in the United Kingdom to apples that were imported to the United Kingdom from New Zealand. Though the New Zealand apples had a higher number of food miles, the study found that they actually had lower embodied energy. They were responsible for fewer greenhouse gas **emissions** than the British apples. In sunny New Zealand, the apple trees are much more productive than those in the United Kingdom.

Because of this, they require less energy to grow. The New Zealand apples did travel thousands of miles across the ocean, but shipping is a fairly energy-efficient transportation method.

It can be difficult for even a well-informed shopper to know which foods are the greenest. Many times, food labels do not indicate where the food was grown, the methods used to grow it, or how the farmworkers were treated. Some companies do label their products to give you this information, but these foods may be too expensive for many families to buy.

The best thing a consumer can do is to learn about the issues surrounding food production, consider the options, and make decisions based on this knowledge and his or her budget. The following sections will give you information about the issues surrounding different types of food to help you make the best choices for you and your family.

Tropical fruits are grown in many less developed countries. Fair trade labels indicate fair payments to workers.

Fruits and Vegetables

Section Summary

Fruits and vegetables are the main part of any healthy diet. Buying fresh fruits and vegetables from local farms is one way to go green. However, buying canned and frozen foods allows you to eat these foods when they are not in season.

Organic foods have been grown without the use of synthetic chemicals. These foods are often more expensive than conventional choices, but they may offer health and environmental benefits. If you are on a tight budget, you can look into which foods are grown with large amounts of synthetic chemicals and choose organic options for only these foods.

Farmers' markets offer locally grown, seasonal fruits and vegetables.

Fresh fruits and vegetables are the foods that fit most easily into a green lifestyle. Many people have access to local growers at farm stands and farmers' markets. Even in supermarkets, fresh produce tends to be sold loose, or with minimal packaging.

Seasonal options

Vegetables and fruits are best when they are fresh and in season. When you buy from a farmer, you know the food was harvested recently. If you shop at a supermarket, you have to know when certain vegetables and fruits are in season. Reading the label can give you clues. For example, if asparagus came from Mexico and you are in Ohio, asparagus is probably not in season in Ohio.

When **perishable** produce is stored for a long time, it is usually refrigerated, which uses energy. Another method involves harvesting produce early and storing it in a special chamber filled with a gas that prevents ripening. Later, another gas causes the produce to ripen right before it goes to market. Such food has less nutritional value, along with poorer taste and texture.

Before you shop, check which foods are in season in your region. The Natural Resources Defense Council, a U.S.-based envi-

Canned items allow for more food options the year around.

ronmental organization, provides a month-to-month list of seasonal foods for each state at www.nrdc.org/health/foodmiles.

Production methods

Some people prefer the taste and potential health benefits of **organic** food. Others purchase the organic option only for foods that are usually grown with large amounts of **pesticides**. Such items include apples, peaches, strawberries, cherries, bell peppers, lettuce, and celery. The Environmental Working Group tracks pesticide **residues** in produce. You can check their Food News Web site (www.foodnews.org) for up-to-date listings.

Processed fruits and vegetables

You can also buy fruits and vegetables frozen, canned, or dried. Such foods carry higher **embodied energy** than fresh produce due to additional processing and packaging. However, the processing allows you to eat produce out of season. Canned and frozen produce sometimes have even more nutrients than fresh produce.

Dried fruits are often sold **in bulk**, which eliminates extra packaging. Vitamin C tends to be reduced in the drying process, but many nutrients are preserved. However, dried fruits can have added sugar or substances to which some people are allergic.

Fruits and Vegetables   35

A CLOSER LOOK
Heirloom Varieties

Many small farmers and gardeners are working to increase **biodiversity** and improve flavor by growing heirloom varieties of fruits and vegetables. The seeds for these plants have been carefully preserved and passed from one gardener to another, sometimes for more than a century. Heirloom varieties may look quite different from more common varieties. For example, there are tomatoes that stay green when they are fully ripe or that have dark purple flesh. There are cucumbers that look like lemons on the outside. The Seed Savers Exchange (www.seedsavers.org) was established in 1975 to provide a way for growers to trade their heirloom seeds.

Meat and Poultry

Section Summary

Meat and poultry products are often produced by large commercial farms. The animals may be kept in small feedlots. They are often fed corn, which is not part of their natural diet. They may also be fed antibiotics to keep them healthy.

Some farmers raise livestock on pastures so the animals can eat their natural diet. These animals usually require few or no antibiotics.

Such labels as "organic," "grass-fed," "pasture-raised," and "cage-free" can help you determine how the animals you eat were treated and what they were fed.

Commercial chicken farms confine thousands of animals in tiny spaces.

It is greener to eat plants than foods derived from domestic animals that eat plants. Some people call this eating "low on the **food chain**." Plants are at the bottom of the food chain and get their energy from the sun, while animals must feed on plants or other animals. Meat and poultry have greater environmental impact because farmers must first grow crops for animal feed. After that, more resources are needed to raise the animals and process the meat or other products. One way of dealing with this problem is to become a vegetarian, but many people insist on eating meat. For those who prefer to be **carnivores** (meat-eaters), it is still possible to make greener choices with the meats you buy.

CAFO's and animal health

On industrial-scale farms, livestock are kept in large **feedlots** called concentrated animal feeding operations, or CAFO's. The animals live close together and may be indoors. Egg-laying chickens are grouped wing-to-wing in small cages called batteries. The manure, droppings, and other wastes from CAFO's can escape into **ground water**, polluting the environment. Because diseases travel quickly in cramped quarters, the livestock get sick more easily.

Some animals become irritable in crowded pens. Many poultry

farmers cut off the tips of chickens' beaks to keep them from pecking one another. Pig farmers often remove, or

Livestock kept in crowded feedlots must be fed antibiotics to prevent disease.

"dock," their animals' tails to keep other pigs from biting them.

CAFO feed

Livestock in CAFO's do not eat the foods their bodies evolved to process. Cattle, for example, naturally graze on grass. Chickens naturally scratch in the ground for insects and seeds. Livestock in CAFO's, however, are fed specially formulated feed. The most common feed for all animals is corn. In addition to corn, feed typically contains vitamins, **antibiotics**, and meat **by-products**.

The purpose of specially formulated feed is to make animals grow fast and large, not necessarily to help them be healthy. Cattle that eat much corn are vulnerable to health problems, which are usually treated with antibiotics. An estimated 70 percent of the antibiotics used in the United States each year are given to livestock. **Hormones** are also used on cattle to make them bigger.

Alternatives to CAFO's

Farmers who focus on **organic** methods try to allow their animals to live more naturally. They let their livestock spend time outside, with room to move. They work to prevent diseases so fewer medications are needed. They plan for their animals to take a longer amount of time to mature, and they do not use **synthetic** chemicals to speed the process.

Burning cow carcasses

In recent years, the American bison has become a increasingly popular alternative to traditional livestock.

Free-range animals

Animals raised outdoors are described as being "pasture-raised" or "free-range." Such grazing livestock as cattle and lambs are said to be "grass-fed." Ideally, they eat only grass as long as it is available and receive hay in winter. Poultry, such as chickens and turkeys, are cage-free. They, too, spend time out in the pastures, eating a natural diet of bugs, worms, and seeds. Pigs can forage outdoors for grass, roots, and such nuts as acorns. On organic farms, the fields are free of banned substances. All additional feed, such as the cows' hay or the grains given to chickens and pigs, is organically grown.

Australia and some South American countries, notably Brazil, Uruguay, and Argentina, are large producers of free-range beef and other meats. These countries have vast areas of grasslands.

Pasture raising animals is considered less environmentally damaging and more humane than the industrial methods used by CAFO's. Pasture raising can also help to save some kinds of animals that might otherwise have disappeared. Farmers are reviving traditional breeds of livestock that thrive on a natural diet. The American bison, a wild relative of cattle that was hunted almost to extinction in the late 1800's, is gaining popularity as a meat source, so the population is rising. Many farmers give bison a free-range lifestyle.

Shopping for meat and poultry

Organic and free-range meats cost more than conventional meats. However, they are gaining popularity with people who wish to promote more humane treatment of animals and discourage the use of antibiotics and hormones in farming. Both substances, along with other **agrochemicals**, have made their way into the environment in the runoff from large farms and are harming wildlife. Although there are not supposed to be traces of hormones in meat if they are administered properly, many worry that food does get contaminated. For children, exposure to hormones can interfere with the body's development. For adults, hormones may increase the risk of developing certain cancers.

The main trouble with antibiotics is the frequency with which farmers use them. Since harmful **bacteria** develop resistance to antibiotics when they are used repeatedly, unnecessary use of antibiotics can help create new strains of bacteria that resist treatment with medication.

Buying meat from a butcher shop or directly from a farmer allows customers to talk to the seller and find out how the meat was produced. If you do shop at the supermarket meat department, be sure to read the label on meat products. Try to buy meat the day it was packed, and make sure it looks fresh. Take care to cook meat thoroughly according to package directions to kill harmful organisms that could possibly be present, such as salmonella and *E. coli* bacteria.

Farmers' markets allow customers to ask how the food was produced.

Dairy Products and Eggs

Section Summary

Dairy products in the United States often come from cows that are given hormones to increase milk production. This practice can makes cows more vulnerable to disease, so they may also treated with antibiotics. If you wish to avoid added hormones and antibiotics in your milk, look for organic milk products.

Eggs often include numerous labels that can be confusing to consumers. However, the organic label is one of the most reliable.

Many countries have banned use of synthetic hormones in dairy products.

Dairy products

Conventional farms that raise dairy cattle often give their animals the **synthetic hormone** rBGH (recombinant bovine growth hormone), also known as rBST, to increase milk production. As a result, dairy cows have a tendency to contract an udder infection called mastitis and are then treated with **antibiotics.** When antibiotics are overused, **microbes** can develop a resistance to them, causing stronger strains of **bacteria** to develop.

Hormones control many body activities, including growth, development, and reproduction. Some studies have shown that the use of hormones in cattle may cause early-onset puberty in girls. Synthetic hormone levels in milk may also cause higher rates of certain cancers.

Use of synthetic hormones is banned in such countries as Canada, Japan, Australia, and some countries of the **European Union.** However, they are widely used by dairy farms in the United States. In some U.S. states, it is illegal for milk products to have hormone-free labels because some feel that such labels imply that milk products that contain hormones are not safe.

If you wish to avoid added hormones in your milk, you can buy milk directly from small dairy farmers committed to **sustainable** methods. You can also choose items that are labeled "**organic.**" Organic milk must meet U.S. federal standards, so you can count on a certain level of quality. However, several different producers usually are involved in getting milk products from farms to grocery stores, and lapses in quality can occur. Most dairy brands establish **cooperatives**. That is, the brands buy milk from many farmers to be used in the products sold under the brand name, such as milk, yogurt, butter, or ice cream.

Eggs

You will find many claims on egg packages—and sometimes more than one at a time—but organic label is the most reliable. It would be illegal for sellers to lie when using other labels, but sometimes facts are interpreted in ways you might not expect. The chart below lists common labels found on egg cartons and their meaning.

When purchasing eggs, you can also consider the type of packaging. Paper egg cartons are **biodegradable** and are a better choice than nonbiodegradable plastic or polystyrene.

Egg Package Labels	
If the carton says...	It means...
Organic	The farm and the eggs meet USDA organic standards.
Pasture-raised or grass-fed	The hens spent time in movable pens placed in pastures. These eggs are likely available only from small farmers.
Free-range or free-roaming	The hens had access to the outdoors, but no set amount of time is specified, nor is there a standard for what the outdoor area should be like.
Cage-free	The hens were allowed to roam indoors. There are no standards for what sort of area this should be.
Vegetarian	The hens were never given feed that contains meat products.
Antibiotic-free or hormone-free (or similar wording)	Neither claim requires **certification.** Also, synthetic hormones are not usually used for egg-laying chickens, so nearly all eggs are hormone-free.

Seafood

Section Summary

Seafood is an important part of many people's diet. However, the demand for seafood has damaged fish and shellfish populations, bringing some close to extinction. Pollution of the oceans and rivers has also damaged these populations.

People have developed fish farms to raise fish for food. Many people believe that fish farming will help make the fishing industry fully sustainable.

To purchase seafood that is considered sustainable and safe to eat, use the Internet to research the latest information on fish populations.

Commercial fishing fleets have driven many kinds of fish to the edge of extinction.

Humans were catching and eating fish before they learned to grow crops. Highly nutritious and protein-filled, seafood is still a major part of people's diet in many cultures, particularly in Asia and Africa. The world demand for seafood has led to large numbers of sea creatures being killed, bringing many species close to extinction. Pollution of the oceans and rivers has also damaged these populations. As a result, there is a strong move to develop **sustainable** methods of producing seafood.

Wild seafood

Fish caught in the wild have led natural lives, and no human resources were used to raise them. Unfortunately, natural sources of seafood are becoming dangerously depleted.

As in agriculture, technological improvements have made it possible to harvest large numbers of fish and shellfish at once. Large, cone-shaped nets called trawls are dragged behind boats to scoop fish out of the water. Mesh sacks called dredges are dragged along the sea floor to capture shellfish. Gillnets are positioned like fences in the water to snag fish swimming past. Another net wall is set up around a school of fish and tightened until the whole crowd can be pulled onto the boat.

These methods of catching fish and shellfish have caused dramatic reductions in some fish populations. In some instances, there might not be enough of the targeted species left to replenish the population. And many other creatures—sea turtles, sharks, dolphins, and sea birds, to name only a few—are killed as **bycatch**. The number of animals hauled in by **commercial** fishers as bycatch varies from about 15 percent to as much as 90 percent.

Farmed fish

Fish farming, or aquaculture, is the practice of raising fish for food. Right now, it provides about 40 percent of the world's seafood. Aquaculture is ideal for fish and shellfish that are **herbivores** (plant-eaters) and can reproduce in captivity, such as catfish, tilapia, mussels, and clams. Many fish, however, are **carnivores**, such as salmon. They are fed ocean-caught fish, which helps to destroy wild populations.

Aquaculture can also damage the environment. Fish held in pens in the ocean sometimes escape, potentially impacting wild fish populations. Waste from pens can pollute the water, and diseases can spread from the farmed fish into the wild.

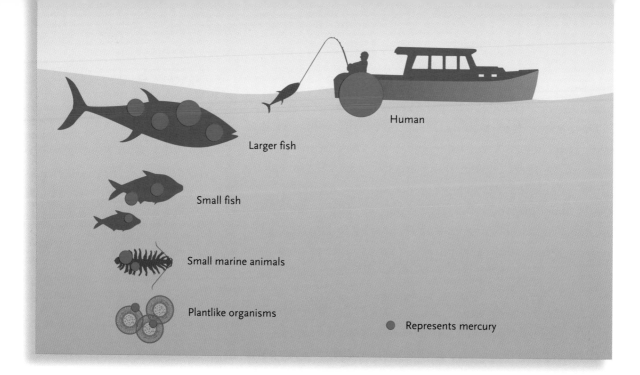

As large fish eat small ones, such toxins as mercury become concentrated.

Mercury in seafood

Pollution has become an increasing problem in oceans and other bodies of water. **Pollutants** in water tend to spread upward through the **food chain.** As a result, toxic chemicals can become concentrated in the bodies of fish high in the food chain.

Mercury is a **heavy metal** that contaminates rivers and oceans. Some mercury is released naturally during undersea volcanic activity. However, power plants and chemical refineries release large amounts of mercury as a pollutant. Mercury is highly toxic to humans and can cause severe brain damage and paralysis (inability to move) in high doses. The fish with the highest levels of it are such wild-caught large predators as sharks, swordfish, and some tunas. These fish live a long time, and it is difficult for the body to rid itself of mercury. Large predators become more contaminated with mercury with each fish they eat.

In the past decade, reports of seafood contamination have raised fears about the safety of eating certain types of fish. In 2004, the FDA urged pregnant and nursing women to stop eating certain ocean fish, such as shark, mackerel, swordfish, tilefish, and albacore tuna. Mercury is especially harmful to infants and children, as it interferes with brain and nerve development.

Generally speaking, the nutritional benefits of seafood often outweigh the risks. Seafood contains high levels of omega-3 fatty acids, which protect against heart disease and other diseases.

However, it is a good idea to avoid some types of fish or to eat them in moderation. Pregnant women, nursing mothers, and children should eat seafood that tends to be low in mercury, such as shrimp, salmon, pollock, catfish, and canned light tuna.

Shopping for seafood

When shopping for seafood, read labels to help you choose sustainable options. A U.S. federal "country-of-origin" law was passed in 2002 requiring retailers to label seafood so you know where it comes from and how it was raised. The law is being put into effect slowly, so you may need to ask your grocer to begin providing this information.

Even with the labels, you will need to do some research on your own to know what to choose. The status of fish populations changes regularly. The Monterey Bay Aquarium (www.mbayaq.org) publishes a Safe Seafood Guide that focuses on sustainability. You will find information about contaminant levels in the Seafood Selector from the Environmental Defense Fund (www.edf.org). Both guides can be printed out so you can carry them with you to a store or restaurant.

As fish populations plunge, green seafood choices may save some species.

In the 1950's, many tuna fishers found schools of tuna by looking for the dolphins that swam along with them at the water's surface. The fishers would then net the tuna, often catching nearby dolphins as well. As many as 100,000 dolphins were killed this way every year.

In 1986, the Earth Island Institute, a U.S.-based environmental organization, organized a tuna **boycott** to protest this practice. In 1997, President Bill Clinton signed into law the International Dolphin Conservation Program Act, which controlled fishing methods. Now around 90 percent of canned tuna brands follow those rules, and dolphin deaths from tuna fishing have dropped to about 2,000 a year. These products bear a logo that reads "Dolphin Safe."

U.S. Department of Commerce
Dolphin Safe

Seafood   45

Beans and Grains

Section Summary

Beans and grains are often sold as canned or frozen goods in grocery stores. Some stores sell dried beans and grains in bulk. This allows shoppers to choose how much they want to buy and cuts down on packaging waste. Organic versions are available for most beans and grains.

Beans and grains are often sold loose, reducing packaging and waste.

Beans belong to the plant family known as legumes. Some legumes, such as peas, may be eaten fresh, but they can also be dried. This process preserves them for long periods of time. Beans have a high protein content, so they are a great choice for vegetarians. Unlike meat, they also provide beneficial dietary fiber. Examples of beans include pinto beans, navy beans, garbanzo beans, and split peas.

Dried beans do not require much more packaging than a plastic bag. If you can buy them **in bulk**, you will not only avoid packaging, but probably will pay an economical price. Many beans are available canned; they usually contain added salt. Some beans, such as black-eyed peas and lima beans, are available frozen.

Soy and soy products

The soybean is one of the most versatile of all foods. First cultivated in China at least 3,000 years ago, it is a staple of Chinese and Japanese cuisines. It is popular around the world in many

GREEN FACT

Quinoa (*KEE noh ah*) is a grain plant native to the Andes Mountains of South America that is gaining popularity in many countries because of its nutritional value. Both the seeds and the leaves of the quinoa are rich in protein and other nutrients.

forms. Soy provides all the proteins you need, and it contains vitamins and beneficial **antioxidants.** Among the products made from soybeans are oil, soy sauce, tofu, snacks, and an astonishing variety of dairy and meat substitutes—soy made to mimic milk, yogurt, ice cream, sausages, cold cuts, and versions of beef and chicken. Soybeans can also be eaten fresh, in which case they are called edamame. Many soy products are processed and packaged, which represent high **embodied energy.**

Soy is an important part of many people's diet, but soy farming in some parts of the world has led to environmental damage. Farmers in Brazil have cleared large areas of the Amazon rain forest to grow soy crops. Much of this soy is used for animal feed and industrial purposes. Read package labels or contact the manufacturers to ask if **sustainable** farming methods were used.

Grains

Grains are the seeds or tiny fruits of cereal grasses, such as rice, wheat, oats, and corn. Like beans, whole grains are sold in simple packaging or in bulk. Grains are also ground up into flours and used to make breads or breakfast cereals. However, many breakfast cereals are highly processed and have higher embodied energy than whole grains.

If you wish to avoid **genetically modified** foods, it is best to buy **organic** corn and soybean products. Many conventional farmers in the United States grow genetically modified varieties of these crops. Organic standards forbid the use of genetically modified crops, however.

Soybeans, below, can be made into a dazzling variety of food products, above.

Chocolate and Coffee

Section Summary

Chocolate and coffee producers often clear tropical forests to make room for farming. In addition, farmworkers in countries that grow these items may not be paid a fair wage.

When shopping for chocolate and coffee, check for labels that indicate the farming practices used and the treatment of the farmworkers.

Conventional coffee farms can devastate forests and wildlife.

The Fairtrade certification label

Before you buy chocolate or coffee, remember that, depending on where you live, the raw materials may have been shipped from far away, and can represent many **food miles.** If you want them anyway (and many people do), consider ways to make the greenest choices possible.

Fair trade products

Both coffee and cacao come from less developed countries. The growers make very little money, especially compared to what consumers pay for the luxuries of eating chocolate and drinking coffee. Just as some organizations have addressed the products' environmental effects, others have focused on the social effects.

In 1997, a variety of international groups concerned with the ethical treatment of workers joined together to create Fairtrade Labelling Organizations International (FLO), based in Germany. FLO members establish fair standards and provide **certification** to help consumers identify qualified products.

Coffee and chocolate are well known for their availability with fair trade certification, but other foods and goods can be certified, too. Buying fair-trade products ensures that workers receive a fair wage for growing these goods.

Shade-grown products

Both coffee and cacao (the chocolate plant) grow in tropical climates. Brazil and Indonesia produce most of the world's coffee and some chocolate. Most chocolate comes from West Africa. Until the 1970's, both crops were cultivated on a small scale, often in the shade of a rain forest. Crops grown without destroying forests are called shade-grown.

Hoping to profit more from conventional methods, growers began clearing the forests and converting to sun-tolerant coffee and cacao. Worries about **deforestation** and **global warming** were not yet widespread, but eventually, bird watchers in North America observed that songbird populations were declining. They began to wonder if this was caused by loss of forest in the tropics, where the birds spent the winters. On the farms, people noted that wildlife disappeared, the soil was more easily depleted of nutrients, and **erosion** had increased.

Conservationists began working to convince growers to return to more **sustainable** methods. When growers heed this advice, many negative environmental effects are reversed.

Shopping for coffee and chocolate

Various seals and logos related to ethical concerns are used on coffee and chocolate. As a result, it can be difficult to decide which is most important. Ideally, you want something **organic**, fair trade, *and* shade-grown. However, you may not often find items with such "triple certification."

The organic label may be less important than the other labels. Shade-grown coffee and cacao are likely close to organic. In that setting, fewer **pesticides** are used because birds and bats eat harmful insects. Most likely, the farmers do not use sophisticated machines or **agrochemicals**. Harvests are usually done by hand. Although fair trade certification does not cover the same issues as shade-grown, it does include some environmental provisions.

Fair-trade labels help protect workers, such as this woman harvesting cacao in Ghana.

Where to Shop

Section Summary

Where you shop for food can impact your food choices. Large supermarkets and local grocery stores sell a variety of items. Food cooperatives are grocery stores owned by members. They often sell local foods and health foods.

Farmer's markets are open seasonally in many cities and towns. Some farmers who attend these markets offer community supported agriculture (CSA) subscriptions. With such subscriptions, customers pay in advance for a share of a farm's harvest, which they pick up at designated locations.

Supermarkets are efficient, but their green food options can be limited.

Making green decisions about food may take some practice. Luckily, as more people join the effort, your choices increase. There are many places and ways to shop for food, some of which are explored on the following pages.

Supermarkets

Supermarkets are large grocery stores that carry a variety of foods and household products. They are accessible to most everyone, and they allow you to buy most of what you need in one place. This alone is green—the less you drive, the better.

Organic and local choices in supermarkets may be limited, though. Some people worry that mass-produced organic foods that are shipped long distances do not meet the goals of **sustainable** production.

If you wish to purchase organic, sustainable food, the best way to do so is to stay informed. Learn which organic brands have the highest standards and support them. Ask your grocer to supply more local foods. Companies offer more sustainable choices if customers insist. Nearly $22 billion was spent around the world on organic foods in 2002. By 2007, that amount had grown to almost $44 billion. Even the largest supermarket chains—Wal-Mart in the United States, Carrefour in France, and Tesco in the United Kingdom—offer organic products.

Independent grocery stores run by local owners may feature more local items than large chains, and they often respond to customers' requests. Food **cooperatives**, or co-ops, focus on sustainable and local foods. Co-ops are owned by their members, who pay a fee to join and may occasionally work at the store. Many co-ops allow nonmembers to shop there, but they will pay higher prices than members.

Farmers' markets

When you buy from farmers, you help ensure that they receive a fair living and contribute directly to the production of the next crop. Little or no money is wasted on advertising, packaging, or long-distance shipping.

Some farmers operate farm stands. For a few crops, such as berries, pumpkins, and apples, farmers may open "you-pick" operations, where customers can directly harvest produce.

At farmers' markets, growers meet at a scheduled place and time to sell to the public. Unlike farm stands, which are in rural areas, farmers' markets are often located in cities.

CSA farm shares

Another good choice for city-dwellers is a community supported agriculture (CSA) subscription. With CSA, customers pay in advance for a share of a farm's harvest, which is planned to offer good variety. Then, over the growing season, customers pick up their produce at a designated spot, or they get home delivery every week or two. The Local Harvest Web site (www.localharvest.org) maintains a directory of CSA's in the United States.

One difficulty with buying from farmers is having to adjust your shopping list according to the season and to what the farmer decides to grow. Some people cannot afford to pay upfront for a CSA—the charge may be several hundred dollars for one to three seasons' worth of food. For others, the gas needed to drive to the country cancels any environmental benefits. During winter, most stands and farmers' markets close.

Visiting a "you-pick" farm can be a fun way to learn about the harvesting process.

Green Practices at Home

Section Summary

Green practices at home involve making the most of the food you buy. Avoid creating food waste whenever possible. Instead, refrigerate or freeze leftovers. You can also learn to compost food. Composting is a process where food breaks down into rich nutrients that can be used for fertilizer.

Reusing and recycling is an important kitchen practice. For example, you can purchase a reusable cloth shopping bag to cut down on your waste. You can also recycle glass, plastic, and metal food containers.

Making green choices at home can greatly reduce waste.

What you do with your groceries after you bring them home has an impact on the environment. Consider the ideas presented below for green practices in the kitchen, and stay on the lookout for new ones, too.

Reducing food waste

Throwing away food creates waste on many levels:

- You lose money.
- You waste the resources that were used to grow, prepare, package, and transport the food to market.
- You miss out on the energy it would have supplied to you if you had eaten it.
- Food thrown in the trash wastes yet more energy when it is transported to the garbage dump, and it contributes to overcrowding in **landfills.**
- Food ground up in a garbage disposal unit uses much water. It also adds to the burden on public or private water treatment systems, which process household wastewater.

To address these problems, try to figure out how much food you need before you go shopping. Always store food properly so it lasts until you eat it, and when you do have leftovers, remember to eat them. If you have a lot of extra food that is still good, consider taking it to a food bank or homeless shelter.

Composting

If you have the time and patience, **composting** is an ideal way to handle food waste. Compost, also called humus, is created by a natural process called fermentation, along with other actions from such beneficial **organisms** as earthworms and certain **bacteria**. The process breaks down plant matter—such as coffee grounds and fruit and vegetable scraps—into a dark, fragrant material that can be used as garden **fertilizer.**

Unfortunately, you cannot put meat, fish, dairy, or oily substances into most compost piles. It is also better to have a yard where you can build a compost pile, as well as a garden to make use of the compost. However, some people compost entirely indoors, using a special bin with a tightly fitting lid.

One downside of composting is that it can become quite smelly. Indoor composting in particular must be tended properly in order to prevent foul-smelling odors from taking over the house. There are electric indoor composters that speed the composting process and reduce odors. These devices cost around $250 or more and use electric power.

Freezing foods

Freezing foods is a great way to stock up while produce is in season so you can enjoy it later on. Freezing works well with cooked foods or foods you intend to cook. The low temperature keeps harmful **microbes** from multiplying, so the food will not spoil as long as it remains cold. Fruits and meats can be frozen without any cooking. It is good to drop vegetables briefly in boiling water first. An added benefit is that keeping a well-stocked refrigerator-freezer compartment helps make your refrigerator more energy-efficient, too.

The process of freezing changes the texture of foods, so cheese and such tender vegetables as lettuce or celery are usually not suitable for freezing. Wrap foods to be frozen in foil or seal them in a plastic bag or container. This will help keep them from absorbing unpleasant flavors or getting freezer burn (discolored dry spots). Label packages with the food type and date to keep your stock organized.

Composting food scraps can generate rich fertilizer that is perfect for home gardens.

Using cloth bags instead of plastic bags saves energy and space at landfills.

Canning foods

Canning involves cooking food to kill the microbes that cause spoilage. The food is then sealed inside sterilized glass jars or metal cans. Home cooks use glass jars sterilized by boiling water.

It is best to limit your first canning projects to fruits and vegetables, which can either be minimally cooked or made into such items as jams, jellies, pickles, and sauces. Be sure to work with an experienced canner, consult a reliable cookbook, and follow the directions carefully. Improperly canned foods can spoil or become extremely poisonous.

Reusing and recycling

There are many ways to reuse and recycle in the kitchen. Re-sealable sandwich or freezer bags can be used several times and are easy to wash by hand. Purchase a reusable glass or aluminum drink bottle and refill it regularly rather than buying disposable water bottles.

It is especially important to make green choices in how you bring your groceries home. Purchase a reusable cloth bag instead of taking disposable plastic or paper bags from stores. Each year, making paper bags consumes huge volumes of water and millions of trees, contributing to **deforestation.** Americans throw away around 100 billion plastic bags every year, many of them after only minutes of use. Millions of plastic bags are now floating in the world's oceans, doing great harm to wildlife.

You can further reduce waste by avoiding single-serving items. Instead, buy large packages or buy **in bulk** and portion the food into reusable containers at home. You can also reuse the thin plastic bags that hold produce, such as lettuce or broccoli.

Before you throw out food packaging, check to see if you can recycle it. Many cities offer curbside recycling pickup along with garbage collection. Learn what the rules are for your area. Which items can be recycled? Do you have to sort or bundle them? Can beverage cans be returned to the store for a refund of the deposit?

Gardening

Planting a garden is a great way to reduce your environmental impact and to feel connected to your food supply. It also allows you to cultivate the foods you like best, using **sustainable** methods. You will get to taste the food when it is at its best and most nutritious, just after harvest.

In cities, many people who do not have their own yards participate in community gardens, which are usually constructed in vacant urban lots with the permission of the land owner or city government. In Europe, similar gardens are known as "allotment gardens." The available land is divided into plots that are rented out to interested gardeners in the area.

Try to make green choices as you garden. Make and use compost for fertilizer. Set up a barrel to collect rainwater so you need less water from a faucet. Limit the driving you do to get gardening supplies. Some gardeners become so successful that they produce more food than they can eat. If this happens to you, maybe you can set up a small vegetable stand of your own.

Many cities have begun to sprout gardens on the rooftops of buildings, such as this one in Thailand.

Going Green at School

Section Summary

Going green at school involves promoting green practices. If you eat in a school cafeteria, talk with teachers and students about ways to green your school cafeteria's practices and food options. If you bring your own lunch, use reusable food containers and minimize your food and packaging waste.

School cafeterias around the world have started to go green. Some schools plant gardens and prepare meals from their harvests. Other schools serve organic meals and recycle food waste.

Schools have become leaders in promoting sustainable food choices.

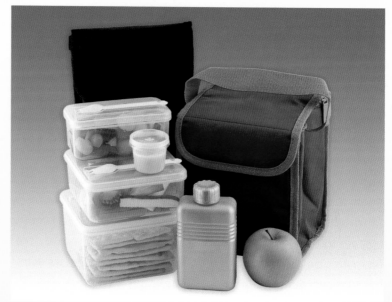

Many school students eat lunch in cafeterias that offer few green options for dining. However, a number of people are working to improve this situation.

Berkeley's School Lunch Initiative

Berkeley, California, is a hotspot for **sustainable** food practices. An influential figure in the sustainable foods movement named Alice Waters lives there. Waters opened a restaurant, Chez Panisse, in 1971, focusing on seasonal, local foods. In 1996, she established a foundation to promote education about food in public schools. In the Edible Schoolyard project, middle school students plant and tend a garden, then prepare meals from their harvests as part of the curriculum. For her School Lunch Initiative, Waters helped to hire a chef, Ann Cooper, who is now the director of the Berkeley public school lunch program. Although Cooper must work within rules set by National Lunch Program laws, she has removed processed foods from menus and introduced fresh and **organic** options.

Other green schools

Sustainable practices are being introduced in many other places, too. Many U.S. states have adopted farm-to-school programs, which bring local farmers' produce into lunchrooms. Oklahoma, in particular, has adopted this approach, along with 43 other states.

School gardens, used for both teaching and food production, are increasingly popular. The Organic School Project, initiated by Chicago chef Greg Christian teaches students organic gardening, menu planning, and food preparation. The National Gardening Association keeps an updated database of schools in the United States that have youth gardening programs at www.kidsgardening.com. Many school gardening programs also have **composting** programs to recycle cafeteria waste.

All over the world, there is a move to make school cafeterias greener. In 2000, the Italian government passed a law requiring all schools to serve organic foods. A famous British chef, Jamie Oliver, began a campaign in 2005 to improve school lunches by participating in a reality television show. *Jamie's School Dinners* followed his experiences serving lunch at a school in Greenwich, England. Among the school gardening programs popular in Australia is the Stephanie Alexander Kitchen Garden, in Melbourne. Staff members help grade schools implement the educational programming they have developed.

Greening your school lunches

If your school has not yet made many changes, let teachers and administrators know that you would like to help your school go green. Write articles for the school paper about what can be done, and find out what other schools nearby are doing. You may be surprised at what a difference you can make.

If you bring your own lunch, you are in a good position to make green choices. Pack local, sustainably produced foods rather than heavily processed items and challenge yourself to do it without any disposable packaging. Carry a lunchbox or small cloth tote instead of a paper bag. Wrap foods in wax paper or foil rather than plastic, or put them in reusable containers.

The Jamie Oliver kitchen, below, trains school chefs to cook more nutritious lunches.

Activity
FOOD WASTE AUDIT

Introduction

Sometimes the best way to get an accurate understanding of something is to measure it. If you are not sure how tall you are, you can get out a measuring tape. To understand just how much food waste you generate, conduct a food waste audit (examination) by following the directions below.

Materials:

- Heavy-duty garbage bag for each participant
- 4 containers for garbage (size depends on the number of participants)
- Rubber gloves for handling the garbage
- A scale for weighing the waste

Directions:

1. Decide who is going to be involved in your food waste audit. Will it just be you, or you and a friend? Your whole family? Explain what is involved to the person or persons who will be working with you.

2. Label each of your containers according to what you will put into it. You need labels for (1) wet garbage—**compostable**, (2) wet garbage—not compostable, (3) dry garbage—recyclable, and (4) dry garbage—not recyclable. Be sure to do a bit of investigating so you understand what sorts of items fit into each category of garbage.

Wet Garbage		Dry Garbage	
Compostable	Not Compostable	Recyclable	Not Recyclable
Bread	Meat (red meat, chicken, fish)*	Drink bottles (metal, glass, and most plastic)	Sandwich bags
Fruit scraps, including peels	Dairy Products*	Cardboard and paperboard	Food wrappers, such as plastic wrap
Soup	Paper towels**	Aluminum foil	Potato chip bags
Pasta	Paper napkins**		Candy wrappers
Sauces			
Chips	*These items can be composted, but they can attract rodents and other pests.		
Coffee grounds and tea bags	**If paper towels and napkins do not have chemicals on them, they can be composted.		
Eggshells			

3. Early on the day of the experiment, give each participant a large trash bag. Instruct everyone to save all food-related trash for the whole day. Encourage them to behave just as they normally would. If they usually buy a take-out lunch or snack at a restaurant, they should be sure to do that on this day, too.

4. After your last meal of the day, conduct the audit. Weigh each participant's bag to determine how much trash he or she contributed. Wearing the gloves, sort all the garbage into the containers you prepared. Put each container on the scale and record its weight.

5. Analyze your findings. Questions to ask include:

   - What kind of waste was most common?
   - If other people participated, who accumulated the most trash? Who accumulated the least? Can each explain why?
   - What kinds of waste could have been avoided with a little more planning? What kind of planning would have helped reduce food waste?
   - What could have been done to keep the containers for nonrecyclable and non-compostable garbage emptier—or completely empty?

6. Document your findings and your ideas about how to improve the situation in a report and distribute copies to everybody who helped with your experiment.

7. Consider repeating the audit in a few months, after you have had a chance to practice greener habits. Challenge yourself to reduce your waste to an absolute minimum.

Source: RecycleWorks
(www.recycleworks.org/schools/s_audits.html)

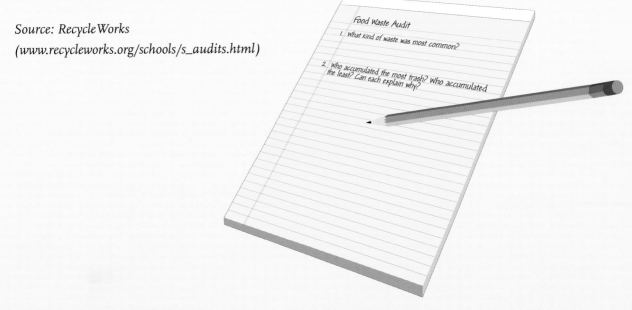

Glossary

additive a substance added in small amounts to something in order to give it certain characteristics.

agribusiness a business that relates in some way to agricultural production.

agrochemical a synthetic chemical used in conventional agriculture.

antibiotic a drug that destroys or weakens germs. Antibiotics are used as medicine to treat infections caused by bacteria.

antioxidant any of a group of chemical compounds that may prevent certain types of cell damage.

atmosphere the mixture of gases in contact with Earth's surface and extending far above.

bacteria a single-celled microbe that lacks a nucleus. Some bacteria cause diseases; others are beneficial.

biodegradable easily decomposed by living things.

biodiversity the amount of variety among plants, animals, and other organisms.

biopesticide a pesticide produced by organisms that makes use of natural biological processes.

boycott a protest in which consumers stop buying a product until their concerns are addressed.

by-product an additional product created in the manufacture of an object or substance.

bycatch unwanted fish and other marine animals caught by fishing boats.

carbon dioxide a colorless, odorless gas given off by burning and by animals breathing out.

carbon footprint the total amount of carbon dioxide given off by a particular human activity.

carbon monoxide a toxic, colorless, odorless gas.

carnivore an animal that feeds chiefly on flesh; a plant that digests insects.

certification; certify to declare something true or correct by an official spoken, written, or printed statement; to provide certification.

commercial having to do with trade or business.

composting the process used to break down yard waste and food scraps into rich fertilizer for gardens and grass.

conservation tillage a method of growing crops with less cultivation of the soil, reducing soil erosion.

conserve; conservation to keep from harm or loss; the management, protection, and wise use of natural resources.

conventional agriculture farming practices that include using human-made chemicals to grow plants.

cooperative an enterprise that operates by group participation and may be group-owned.

cover crop a crop planted between growing seasons that protects the soil surface and restores nutrients.

deforestation the destruction of forests.

embodied energy the total amount of energy required to make a product or to carry out an activity.

emission an airborne waste product.

environmentalist a person who wants to preserve nature and reduce pollution.

erosion gradual wearing away of a surface by wind, rain, ice, or other forces.

European Union (EU) an economic and political organization that includes most of the countries of Europe.

eutrophication the build-up of excessive nutrients in a body of water, causing rapid growth of algae and then depletion of oxygen.

fair trade a label that assures an item was produced by workers who were paid and treated fairly.

farm bill laws in the United States that determine various policies relating to agricultural production.

feedlot an area where livestock are kept until they are large enough to be slaughtered for meat.

fertile able to support growth.

fertilizer a substance that helps plants to grow.

food chain a group of interrelated organisms in which each member of the group feeds upon the one below it and is in turn eaten by the organism above it.

food miles the total distance a food travels in all stages of its production before it is consumed.

fossil fuel underground deposits that were formed millions of years ago from the remains of plants and animals. Coal, oil, and natural gas are fossil fuels.

freight goods carried by a form of transportation.

fungicide a poison that kills fungal pests.

gene a tiny part of cells that help determine how an organism will look and function.

genetically modified changed by the scientific process of altering genes in an organism.

global warming the gradual warming of Earth's surface, believed to be caused by a build-up of greenhouse gases in the atmosphere.

greenhouse effect the process by which certain gases cause the Earth's atmosphere to warm.

greenhouse gas any gas that contributes to the greenhouse effect.

ground water water that pools underground in porous rocks.

hardy able to bear hard treatment; strong.

heavy metal a metal, such as lead, mercury, and arsenic, which can collect in the tissues of organisms and is toxic to most living things.

herbicide a poison that kills weeds.

herbivore an animal that feeds on plants.

hormone a substance produced by an organism that typically affects growth and reproduction.

in bulk unpackaged. Customers usually take the amount they want from a larger stock.

industrialized country a country where historical wealth and advanced development contribute to a relatively high standard of living.

insecticide a pesticide that kills insects.

integrated pest management (IPM) a natural method of controlling pests and weeds that avoids use of agrochemicals.

labor union a workers' group that strives to guarantee fair treatment and fair pay for its members.

landfill a place where trash and other solid waste materials are discarded.

microbe any organism that is too small to be seen without magnification.

migrant labor seasonal workers who move from place to place. Such workers are often immigrants.

monoculture the growth of only one kind of crop.

organic produced by plant or animal activities; organic food is grown or raised without the use of synthetic chemicals.

nonrenewable resources resources that cannot be replenished once depleted, such as fossil fuels.

perishable prone to spoil or decay in little time.

pesticide a poison that kills pests such as insects.

pollutant a single source of pollution.

residue a tiny amount of a substance that remains. Residues are often unwanted.

slash-and-burn agriculture cutting down and burning forests to prepare the land for farming.

subsidy a payment intended to help the recipient do something that is considered important.

subsistence farmer a person who farms primarily to support his or her family rather than to produce goods for sale.

sustainable any practice that adheres to principles of conservation and ecological balance.

sustainable agriculture methods of farming that reduce environmental damage from farming while promoting economic growth and social equality.

synthetic human-made.

tillage the breaking up of the soil for cultivation, usually using a plow.

topsoil the fertile surface layer of the soil.

United Nations an international organization that works for world peace and human prosperity.

Additional Resources

WEB SITES

Cornucopia Institute
http://www.cornucopia.org

An organization that advocates for economic justice for small farms.

Environmental Defense Fund Seafood Selector
http://www.edf.org/page.cfm?tagID=1521

Lists eco-friendly and non-eco-friendly options for seafood.

Environmental Working Group's Food News
http://www.foodnews.org

Features a list of fresh produce, ranked according to the amount of pesticides they are likely to contain.

Local Harvest
http://www.localharvest.org

Helps U.S.-based users locate local farmers' markets, CSA subscriptions, eco-friendly restaurants, and more.

Sustainable Table
http://www.sustainabletable.org

Includes a wealth of information on shopping for and serving sustainable food.

Union of Concerned Scientists
http://www.ucsusa.org/food_and_environment

Supplies the latest information on environmental and health issues concerning agricultural practices.

United Nations Food and Agriculture Organization
http://www.fao.org

A reliable resource for information on global food and agricultural issues.

BOOKS

Chew on This: Everything You Don't Want to Know About Fast Food
by Eric Schlosser and Charles Wilson (Houghton Mifflin, 2006)

Critical Perspectives on Genetically Modified Crops and Food
edited by Susan Gordon (Rosen Publishing Group, 2006)

Fair Trade? A Look at the Way the World Is Today
by Adrian Cooper (Stargazer Books, 2006)

Organic Foods
by Debra A. Miller (Thomson/Gale, 2008)

Overweight America
by Meryl Loonin (Lucent Books, 2007)

Index

DATE DUE

APR 01 2013			

DEMCO 38-297